Original title:
Quilted Winter Memories

Copyright © 2024 Creative Arts Management OÜ
All rights reserved.

Author: Ophelia Ravenscroft
ISBN HARDBACK: 978-9916-94-430-1
ISBN PAPERBACK: 978-9916-94-431-8

Frosted Fabrications

Whispers of frost on windows gleam,
Crafted wonders in a winter dream.
Snowflakes dance with delicate grace,
Nature's art in an icy embrace.

Each pattern tells a tale anew,
Of silent nights and skies so blue.
Beneath the chill, a warmth resides,
In frosted worlds where magic hides.

Hearthside Reflections

By the fire, stories unwind,
In the glow, our hearts aligned.
Embers crackle, shadows play,
Gathered close, we drift away.

Memories wrapped in cozy light,
Echoes of laughter fill the night.
Through every flicker, bonds grow strong,
In hearthside warmth, we all belong.

Frosty Patterns of Togetherness

Frosted trees in a soft embrace,
Nature's quilt of winter's grace.
In chilly air, we find the cheer,
Together, love dispels all fear.

Footprints marked in snow so bright,
Crisp and fresh, a pure delight.
We wander paths, hand in hand,
In frosty patterns, we make our stand.

Layers of Time and Tranquility

Time drapes softly, a gentle sound,
In layers deep, peace can be found.
Moments whisper through the years,
Tranquil echoes, love endears.

Each breath a layer, still and calm,
Wrapped in quiet, a soothing balm.
As seasons shift, we hold the fold,
In timeless layers, stories told.

Cozy Corners of Thought

In the nook of the room, I sit still,
A cup of warm tea, a gentle thrill.
Pages of stories, whispers of light,
The world fades away, it's a perfect night.

Blankets wrapped tight, a sweet embrace,
Thoughts drift like clouds, a slow-paced race.
Memories linger, soft as a sigh,
In cozy corners, my spirit can fly.

Soft Shadows on Snow

In the hush of the morning, time slows down,
Soft shadows dance on the blank canvas brown.
Footprints tell stories, a journey begun,
While the world whispers secrets, just to the sun.

Gentle flakes fall, a tender embrace,
Each one unique, nature's own lace.
The crisp winter air fills my lungs with cheer,
Soft shadows remind me that spring will be here.

Binds of the Past

Tales woven tight, like threads in a quilt,
Echoes of laughter, and soft dreams built.
Moments remembered, both bitter and sweet,
In the binds of the past, our stories repeat.

Old photographs fade, but feelings stay bright,
Lessons we cherish, like stars in the night.
Time may move on, yet here I remain,
Tied to the roots, through joy and through pain.

Patterns in the Snow

Each flake that falls dances to the ground,
Creating patterns, so unique, so profound.
Nature's brush strokes, a canvas of white,
Whispers of winter awaken the night.

Traces of critters, a story unfolds,
In the silent expanse where the magic beholds.
Footprints of wanderers, hopes left behind,
Patterns in the snow, a tapestry designed.

Love in the Layered Silence

In whispers soft, our hearts align,
Each pause a promise, a bond divine.
Through layered silence, our spirits soar,
In every glance, we seek for more.

Wrapped in stillness, the world fades away,
Embracing moments, come what may.
With every heartbeat, the echoes grow,
In the quiet depths, true love we sow.

Chasing Shadows in the Snowfall

Under a sky, so crisp and bright,
We chase the shadows, pure delight.
Footprints linger, soft and slow,
In the hush of winter's gentle glow.

With each snowflake that flutters down,
We laugh and twirl, no hint of frown.
In fleeting moments, our spirits dance,
Chasing shadows in a wintry trance.

The Warmth of Abiding Light

In the glow of dawn, warmth unfolds,
With stories of love, forever told.
Bright rays cascading through every room,
Chasing away the lingering gloom.

Through trials faced, we find our way,
In the light of hope, we choose to stay.
With every sunrise, our dreams ignite,
Together we shine, a beautiful sight.

Heirlooms Woven in Time

Threads of history, woven tight,
Holding memories, pure and bright.
In every stitch, a tale unfolds,
Of love and loss, of wishes bold.

The fabric carries whispers near,
A legacy we hold so dear.
In each moment, we find our role,
Heirlooms cherished, enfolding the soul.

Tales Wrapped in Flannel

In the corner, shadows creep,
Whispers of secrets, softly weep.
Beneath the quilt, warmth resides,
Each stich a memory, love abides.

Fires crackle, stories flow,
Through the fabric, tales we sow.
Sunlight dances on the seams,
Holding close our woven dreams.

Gentle hands that mend and tie,
Heartfelt moments drifting by.
Threads of laughter, threads of tears,
In flannel hugs, we share our years.

When the world outside feels cold,
In this haven, we grow bold.
With every fold, our hearts expand,
Tales wrapped in flannel, hand in hand.

Cozy Whispers of the Past

In the twilight softly sighs,
Memories linger, like fireflies.
Timeless echoes softly call,
Cozy whispers wrap us all.

Golden light through weathered panes,
Carries laughter, joy, and pains.
Familiar scents in the air,
Transport us to moments rare.

Faded photographs on the wall,
Tell of summers, joyful thrall.
Every shadow, every spark,
Illuminates the deep and dark.

Through the years we weave and spin,
In our hearts, the past begins.
With each whisper, stories last,
In cozy dreams, we hold them fast.

Frosted Fabric of Time

Snowflakes drift in silent grace,
Covering the earth's embrace.
Frosted fabric, soft and bright,
Holds the secrets of the night.

Each frozen thread, a tale unfolds,
Of winter nights and hearths of gold.
Wrapped in warmth, we find our way,
In the stillness of the day.

Whispers blend with chilly air,
Finding comfort everywhere.
Through the window, we can see,
Life's tapestry, wild and free.

Time unfolds like winter's snow,
With every flake, the seasons flow.
In the frost, our hopes take flight,
Woven dreams in purest white.

Embroidered Echoes of Childhood

In the garden where we played,
Every flower's bloom displayed.
Stitches vibrant, tales of youth,
Embroidered echoes, timeless truth.

Tattered toys and stories shared,
Moments cherished, hearts laid bare.
Laughter ringing through the air,
A sense of joy beyond compare.

In the dusk, shadows grow long,
Memories hum a gentle song.
Thread by thread, we stitch anew,
With every glance, we find the view.

Holding tight, the past remains,
In our hearts, the joy retains.
Embroidered echoes softly call,
Whispers of childhood, love for all.

Charms of the Frosted Lane

Whispers of snow on the ground,
Crystals twinkle, peace found.
Footprints lace the silvery hue,
Nature's canvas, soft and new.

Branches bow with frosty grace,
Silent magic fills the space.
Breezes carry winter's sigh,
Underneath the pale gray sky.

Buttons and Boughs in Winter

Buttons bright on coats we wear,
Boughs adorned with a frosty flair.
Wardrobes layered, warmth embraced,
In each stitch, love is traced.

Pine scents linger in the air,
Nature's beauty, beyond compare.
While the cold winds swiftly blow,
Together, we find the glow.

The Comfort of Threaded Dreams

In cozy corners, stories weave,
Threaded dreams, we dare believe.
Each knot a tale, each seam a spark,
In soft hues, we chase the dark.

Fingers dance through yarns so bright,
Crafting warmth on chilly nights.
Stitch by stitch, we build our hopes,
Wrapped in fabric, love elopes.

Homegrown Warmth in White

Fields lie blanketed in white,
Homegrown warmth brings pure delight.
Baked bread smells fill the air,
Gathered round, we share and care.

Family laughter, fireside glow,
In winter's chill, our hearts will grow.
Hand in hand through falling snow,
Home is where the warmth will flow.

Patterns of Stillness and Time

In quiet corners, shadows play,
Echoes of whispers fade away.
Moments linger, soft and light,
Framed in the dance of day and night.

Time flows slow, like drifting fog,
Marking paths on an ancient log.
In each heartbeat, stories blend,
Patterns of stillness, without end.

Weaving Yesterdays into Tomorrow

Threads of gold in the tapestry,
Stitching memories, bold and free.
Weaving emotions, joy, and fear,
Crafting the future from yesteryear.

Looms of fate twist and twine,
Every moment, a sacred sign.
With each knot, a tale to tell,
Of love and loss, and wishing well.

Gentle Threads of a Snowy Tale

Silent flakes on a winter's night,
Cover the earth in blankets white.
Whispers of frost on the window pane,
Soft as dreams that call in vain.

Footprints lost in the drifting snow,
Mark the paths where memories flow.
In the hush of a world remote,
Gentle threads of tales they wrote.

Memories Battered by Winter's Breath

In frigid winds, old echoes sigh,
Battered dreams beneath the sky.
Winter's breath, a chilling song,
Reminds us where we still belong.

Frozen moments, sharp and clear,
Carved in ice, they draw us near.
Yet warmth of love ignites the cold,
In quiet hearts, these tales unfold.

Snowbound Keepsakes

Snowflakes dance on winter's breath,
Covering whispers of trees in depth.
Each flake a tale, a promise sealed,
In the white embrace, the world concealed.

Footprints tread on silent ground,
Echoes of laughter, warmth profound.
Memories trapped in ice and frost,
In this stillness, what is lost?

Branches heavy, bending low,
Holding dreams of spring's warm glow.
Nature's pause, a fleeting day,
In this moment, we softly stay.

Memory's Patchwork Pattern

Fabric woven with threads of time,
Each stitch a heartbeat, a little rhyme.
Colors blend in soft array,
Telling stories of yesterday.

In the quilt of life, we find our place,
Patterns shifting with gentle grace.
Moments stitched, both joy and sorrow,
A tapestry unfolds tomorrow.

Faded patches, stories told,
Whispers of love, both young and old.
Every fragment holds a spark,
Illuminating life from dark.

Hidden Stories Beneath the Snow

Beneath the blanket, tales lie deep,
Secrets of the forest, still and steep.
Winter's hush holds whispers near,
Of life that stirs, though not yet clear.

Roots entwined in silent dreams,
Hidden paths with silver seams.
Each layer softens tales of old,
In crystal confines, stories unfold.

Rabbits hop and shadows glide,
Life still breathes and will not hide.
Beneath the snow, the heart beats slow,
Awaiting spring's warm, gentle glow.

The Narrative of the Thawing Ice

The ice begins to crack and flow,
Revealing tales from buried snow.
Water murmurs truths long kept,
As life, awakened, softly crept.

Underneath, the world finds light,
Colors waking from the night.
Each drop a story, each slide a song,
In the dance of thawing, we belong.

The warmth of sun brings life anew,
As branches bud and skies turn blue.
Nature's script unfolds with ease,
In the gentle whisper of the breeze.

Whispers of the Icy Breeze

Through the frost-kissed trees it glides,
Bringing secrets winter hides.
Gentle whispers, soft and light,
Calling dreams in silver night.

Footsteps crunch on powdered ground,
Echoes of a world unwound.
In the chill, our hearts take flight,
Dancing shadows, pure delight.

Twine of Nostalgia and Snow

Snowflakes fall like whispered dreams,
Each one holds a thousand themes.
Memories wrapped in winter's quilt,
Tender moments, slowly built.

Worn-out paths we used to tread,
Are now cloaked in white and red.
Hand in hand, we pause and sigh,
As the past like snow drifts by.

Frozen Stitches of Togetherness

In the cold, our breaths unite,
Warming hearts in frosty night.
Together stitched through time and space,
A tapestry of soft embrace.

Knitted dreams of shared delight,
In every snowflake's gentle flight.
We weave our stories, love entwined,
A tapestry that stays aligned.

Hues of Winter's Embrace

Beneath the sky of grayish hue,
Winter wraps the world anew.
Softly cloaked in sparkling white,
Nature's canvas, pure and bright.

Icicles hang like crystal dreams,
Caught in sunlight's fleeting beams.
Each color sings a silent song,
In winter's arms, we all belong.

Ribbons of Warmth Amidst Cold

Amidst the chill, the fires glow bright,
Ribbons of warmth in the quiet night.
Whispers of comfort, wrapped in light,
Embracing the souls, holding them tight.

A hot cup shared, with stories told,
Fingers entwined, against the cold.
Hearty laughter, as the moments unfold,
Together we stand, brave and bold.

Loom of Laughter and Frost

In the loom of life, laughter weaves,
Frost on the eaves, as winter grieves.
Threads of joy, hold tight our beliefs,
A tapestry twinkling, as memory leaves.

Chilly air, yet smiles abound,
Echoing warmth in the silence found.
Sparkling eyes dance, by joy unbound,
In the heart of winter, love is crowned.

The Embrace of Soft Shadows

Soft shadows linger, as day turns to night,
Embracing the darkness, with gentle light.
Silent whispers weave through the air,
Tales of the heart, cherished and rare.

Moonlight dances on edges of dreams,
In the calm of night, nothing is as it seems.
Every heartbeat echoes, softly it beams,
Wrapped in the fabric of silvered themes.

Ties That Bind Under White Skies

Under white skies, a promise is made,
Ties that bind, never to fade.
Through seasons of change, we bravely wade,
In love's tender hands, our fears are laid.

Footprints in snow, side by side they flow,
Hearts intertwined in the cool morning glow.
With every step, together we grow,
In the warmth of our bond, we brightly stow.

Embracing the Chill

Crisp air whispers softly,
Frosty breaths linger long.
Trees stand bare and lovely,
Nature sings a winter song.

Scarves wrapped tight around necks,
Footprints mark the snow.
Children laugh and connect,
Joy's warmth begins to grow.

Stars sparkle in the night,
The moon casts a silver light.
Embracing the stillness,
As day turns into night.

Fabric of Yesterdays

Threads of gold and silver,
Stitched with care and grace.
Memories rise and quiver,
In this cherished space.

Pictures framed in time,
Echoes of sweet laughter.
Every stitch a rhyme,
Whispers of ever after.

Worn hands gently weave,
Tales of love and loss.
Emotions interleave,
Each moment, a gloss.

Warmth in a Cold Embrace

Fires crackle and pop,
As shadows dance around.
Hearts that never stop,
In the warmth, we're found.

Layers of soft affection,
Beneath a blanket's fold.
Finding sweet connection,
In whispers shared, we're bold.

Cocoa sipped with joy,
Laughter fills the air.
Each moment we enjoy,
Reminds us how we care.

Memories Woven in White

Snowflakes gently fall,
Cloaking all in white.
Nature wears a shawl,
Transforming day to night.

Soft paths tread anew,
Stories left behind.
Each footstep rings true,
In the silence, we're reminded.

Frosted trees stand tall,
Guardians of our past.
In their grace, we call,
Memories that last.

Celestial Threads of Memory

In the night sky, stars align,
Whispers of time, gently entwine.
Each twinkle holds a story told,
In the fabric of dreams, memories unfold.

Echoes of laughter linger near,
Fragments of love, endless and clear.
Time's gentle hand weaves them tight,
In the vast expanse, they sparkle bright.

Beneath the moon's soft, glowing embrace,
We find the past in this sacred space.
Stitched with care, each moment stays,
In celestial threads, they dance and blaze.

Warm Emblems of White Winters

Snowflakes fall like whispered sighs,
Covering earth, where stillness lies.
Each flake a story, unique and light,
Warmth in chill, a breathtaking sight.

Fires crackle with tales of old,
As shadows dance, the night grows bold.
Embers glow with a cozy charm,
In winter's grasp, we feel the warmth.

The world adorned in sheets of white,
Crisp, pure joy in the soft moonlight.
Footsteps crunch on this frozen stage,
A quiet peace, in every age.

Stitches of Unsung Heroes

In the shadows, bravery resides,
Heroes forged where silence abides.
With quiet strength, they face the night,
Their stories woven, out of sight.

Each stitch a struggle, a tale untold,
Resilience shines, pure and bold.
In the fabric of life, they stand tall,
Unsung, yet vital, they answer the call.

Their hands have mended a world of pain,
Threading hope, through loss and gain.
In every act, a legacy grows,
Their truth in the stitches, forever glows.

Frozen Lullabies in the Breeze

Whispers of winter, soft and sweet,
Nature's lullabies, gently repeat.
Through frosted branches, a song takes flight,
Melodies frozen in the still of night.

The wind carries dreams, light as air,
Cradled in silence, everywhere.
Each note a sigh, a gentle tease,
Wrapped in the chill, of winter's freeze.

As snow blankets earth, peace descends,
Frozen lullabies, the heart mends.
In the quiet, the spirit finds ease,
Lost in the magic of winter's breeze.

Echoes in the Icebound Hearth

In winter's grasp, the candles burn,
Whispers of warmth, the shadows turn.
Silent night, the world seems still,
Echoes dance, as time does thrill.

Frosted windows, stories shared,
Memories linger, love is bared.
Through the chill, hearts ignite,
In the hearth, we find our light.

Tucked Beneath the Amber Glow

Underneath the amber hue,
Dreams awaken, skies turn blue.
Gentle breezes, laughter flows,
Moments cherished, love bestows.

Golden fields, a path to roam,
In each corner, we'll find home.
With hands entwined, we softly sway,
Beneath the glow, we'll find our way.

Seasonal Stitches of Love

Springtime blooms with vibrant cheer,
Petals whisper, all is near.
Summer's embrace, warm sun's glow,
Sewn together, hearts will grow.

Autumn leaves in hues of gold,
Stories woven, each is told.
Winter's chill, a quilt so tight,
Seasonal stitches, love's delight.

Secrets Beneath the Starry Skies

Underneath the vast expanse,
We share dreams in whispered chance.
Stars above, a silent guide,
With each secret, worlds collide.

Moonlight spills on tranquil ground,
Promises made without a sound.
In the night, our hearts confide,
Beneath the stars, love's truth can't hide.

Threads of Memory

In the quiet dusk, shadows dance,
Whispers of past take a chance.
Laughter lingers, soft and sweet,
In every corner, a heart's beat.

Seasons change, yet moments stay,
Echoes of joy, the games we play.
Fingers trace through faded seams,
Stitching life with fragile dreams.

Photographs in a worn old book,
Tales of love in every nook.
Time may shift, yet here we bind,
Treasures sealed in heart and mind.

Threads of moments, intertwined,
Comfort found in what we find.
Memory's fabric, rich and bright,
Guiding us through darkest night.

Comforting Stitches of Time

Needles thread through soft delights,
Binding hearts on lonely nights.
Every pull, a promise sewn,
In fabric's warmth, we find our home.

Time bends gently, hugs the past,
Woven tales will ever last.
Stitch by stitch, we weave our lore,
With every knot, we love much more.

Colors bright in twilight's glow,
Soft embrace where we can grow.
In tapestry of smiles and tears,
We find our way throughout the years.

Comfort lies in crafted seams,
In every corner, silent dreams.
Through the stitches, we'll confide,
In this quilt of hearts, we abide.

Cherished Chills

Autumn leaves, a crisp caress,
Whispers cool in nature's dress.
Moments shared, a fleeting thrill,
Cherished chills on a window sill.

Firelight dances, shadows play,
Nostalgic songs of yesterday.
Wrapped in warmth, a soft embrace,
In fleeting time, we find our place.

Snowflakes fall, a silent flight,
Kisses cold, the world in white.
Hot cocoa warms, our laughter blends,
In cherished chills, the heart extends.

Memory's blanket, soft and wide,
Cocooned in dreams where souls reside.
Each tender moment, like the frost,
In time's embrace, we are not lost.

Nostalgic Ties

The threads of youth, a gentle tie,
Binds us still, though years fly by.
In laughter's echoes, memories blend,
Where every journey finds its end.

Old swing sets creak, the past alive,
In simple games, our spirits thrive.
The sound of joy, a timeless song,
Nostalgic ties where we belong.

Photographs faded, edges worn,
Tell of days when love was sworn.
In every smile, a spark ignites,
Binding hearts through endless nights.

With every stitch and woven thread,
In tales of time, we're gently led.
Nostalgic ties, forever strong,
In memory's arms, we all belong.

Cozy Corners of the Heart

In the nook where shadows blend,
Whispers of warmth softly send,
Echoes of laughter and light,
Filling the corners of night.

Cracked leather, books worn and old,
Stories of love waiting to be told,
A flicker of hope, a sigh so deep,
In cozy corners, memories sleep.

Candles flicker, casting their glow,
Illuminating dreams we used to know,
With every heartbeat, a tale unfolds,
In the corners, our life's treasure holds.

We gather here with souls entwined,
In this space, our hearts aligned,
Wrapped in comfort, safe from the cold,
In cozy corners, love will unfold.

Embers Beneath the Snow

Beneath the blanket, white and pure,
Embers of life's warmth endure,
Hidden sparks that softly glow,
In the quiet depths of snow.

Each flake falls with a gentle grace,
Whispers secrets, a silent trace,
Yet underneath, the fire's light,
Keeps the winter's chill from night.

When frost awakens the quiet glade,
We find the warmth that won't fade,
In every drift, a promise found,
Embers beneath, still safe and sound.

So let the world be cold and vast,
We stand by flames that hold us fast,
With hearts alight, together we'll go,
Finding warmth in the fallen snow.

Hushed Melodies in Wool

Wrapped in warmth, the fibers weave,
Hushed melodies, the heart to grieve,
Threads of comfort, soft and light,
Embrace us gently through the night.

With every stitch, a note we play,
A symphony in shades of gray,
Woolen whispers, secrets unfold,
In every fabric, stories told.

As rain taps lightly on window panes,
Hushed melodies weave through the lanes,
In cozy corners, we find our way,
Through woven dreams that softly sway.

A blanket's hug, a knitted lace,
Each thread connects in quiet space,
In woolen warmth, our souls unite,
Singing softly into the night.

Snowflakes on Tattered Fabric

Snowflakes dance on fabric frayed,
In the quiet, their beauty displayed,
Each one a wonder, softly spun,
In tattered cloth, stories begun.

Patterns faded, colors worn,
Yet in the snow, life is reborn,
Threads of memory stitched with care,
Adorned by flakes that grace the air.

Through winter's chill, they gently land,
Creating magic, a fragile band,
On fabric old, they softly play,
A tapestry of night and day.

So let the snowflakes softly fall,
On tattered fabric, we stand tall,
In each small flake, a world anew,
Dancing where dreams and hopes accrue.

Echoes of a Frosty Hearth

In the glow of embers' light,
Flickers dance through winter's night.
Whispers of tales softly unfold,
As warmth wraps around, stories told.

The chill outside bites like a knife,
Yet here we share a cozy life.
Voices hum, with laughter clear,
Echoes linger, drawing near.

Smoke curls high, a gentle sigh,
Binding us with each reply.
Memories built in every crack,
A frosty world we won't look back.

Hearts entwined, a captive spell,
In this haven, all is well.
The hearth ignites both spark and flame,
Together, forever, we remain.

Snippets of a Frozen Past

Frosty windows, icy lace,
Traces left of time and space.
Moments captured, crystal clear,
Frozen whispers, crystal sphere.

Footprints etched in snow so white,
Stories travel through the night.
Echoes of laughter, joy, and pain,
In the stillness, they remain.

Memories dance in winter's glow,
Stitched together, row by row.
Frozen fragments start to thaw,
Revealing life, a silent law.

Every flake a tale to tell,
Of seasons past and all that fell.
As we savor this timeless cast,
We uncover snippets of the past.

The Comfort of Stitched Stories

Threads of memory weave so tight,
In patterns bold, in colors bright.
Each stitch a tale, a path we tread,
In the fabric of life, softly spread.

Laughter echoes in woven seams,
We gather close, wrap up our dreams.
Patches of sorrow, joy, and grace,
Together they form our cherished space.

As seasons change and years unwind,
In every fold, our hearts aligned.
Each tale a comfort, soft and strange,
In stitched stories, we find our change.

With every yarn that we entwine,
We mend the heart, we love, divine.
Creating warmth in every hue,
A quilt of stories, ever new.

A Tapestry of Ice and Warmth

Woven in the chill of night,
A tapestry of black and white.
Frosty colors mix and clash,
In a swirling, vibrant flash.

Textures shift, as shadows play,
In the dance of night and day.
Warmth wraps round, softly hum,
Together, we await what's come.

Silent stories freeze but flow,
In the quiet, feelings grow.
Branches bare, yet holding tight,
Shadows tremble in the light.

This fabric binds both time and fate,
Ice and warmth, we celebrate.
In every thread, we weave our dreams,
A life adorned with endless themes.

Stitches of Frost

In the quiet dawn, frost weaves its thread,
Nature's fingers dance, lightly they tread.
Each blade of grass, a crystal bead,
Whispers of winter, where silence is freed.

Patterns unfold on the window's embrace,
A tapestry spun in the cold's gentle grace.
Life holds its breath, in the chill of the morn,
Footsteps of frost on the fields newly born.

Shimmering pearls hang from tree's boughs bright,
Kissing the earth in the soft morning light.
The world is a canvas of silver and blue,
Stitches of frost telling tales old and true.

As dusk melts away, shadows start to weave,
The whispers of night call, urging to leave.
Yet in the stillness, the magic runs deep,
In the stitches of frost, our dreams softly sleep.

Threads of Silence

In the heart of the night, a stillness unfolds,
Threads of silence weave stories untold.
Stars glimmer softly, the moon hums a tune,
Crickets take refuge, hidden under the moon.

Winds carry secrets, they rustle the leaves,
Nature's own whispers, the heart softly cleaves.
Each breath a connection, to worlds far away,
In threads of silence, our spirits can sway.

Shadows exchange in the cool of the air,
The gentle embrace of a universe rare.
Moments suspended, like dew on the vine,
We find in the silence, that all things align.

Under the canvas of night's velvet hue,
Threads of silence remind us what's true.
In echoes of quiet, our heartbeats resound,
In the tapestry woven, peace can be found.

Whispers Beneath the Snow

Softly it blankets, the world in its glow,
A hush in the valley, whispers beneath snow.
Crystals reflecting the light of the stars,
Stories of winter, carried from afar.

Each flake held a secret of warmth and of chill,
Nature's soft lullaby, the calm and the thrill.
Paths hidden gently, in white drifts so deep,
Whispers beneath snow, where memories sleep.

The air turns electric, with magic unspun,
Footsteps of owls and the dance of the sun.
In each frozen moment, where silence is found,
Whispers beneath snow wrap the world all around.

With the dawn's silver light, the beauty unveils,
A world reborn, as the soft sunlight hails.
From whispers to laughter, life starts to show,
All things awaken from deep beneath snow.

Threads of Silence

In the heart of the night, a stillness unfolds,
Threads of silence weave stories untold.
Stars glimmer softly, the moon hums a tune,
Crickets take refuge, hidden under the moon.

Winds carry secrets, they rustle the leaves,
Nature's own whispers, the heart softly cleaves.
Each breath a connection, to worlds far away,
In threads of silence, our spirits can sway.

Shadows exchange in the cool of the air,
The gentle embrace of a universe rare.
Moments suspended, like dew on the vine,
We find in the silence, that all things align.

Under the canvas of night's velvet hue,
Threads of silence remind us what's true.
In echoes of quiet, our heartbeats resound,
In the tapestry woven, peace can be found.

Whispers Beneath the Snow

Softly it blankets, the world in its glow,
A hush in the valley, whispers beneath snow.
Crystals reflecting the light of the stars,
Stories of winter, carried from afar.

Each flake held a secret of warmth and of chill,
Nature's soft lullaby, the calm and the thrill.
Paths hidden gently, in white drifts so deep,
Whispers beneath snow, where memories sleep.

The air turns electric, with magic unspun,
Footsteps of owls and the dance of the sun.
In each frozen moment, where silence is found,
Whispers beneath snow wrap the world all around.

With the dawn's silver light, the beauty unveils,
A world reborn, as the soft sunlight hails.
From whispers to laughter, life starts to show,
All things awaken from deep beneath snow.

Patchwork Dreams in Frosted Fields

Frost-kissed meadows paint stories anew,
Patchwork of dreams, in each morning dew.
Colors of twilight, a canvas so vast,
Whispers of seasons, each one unsurpassed.

Fields stand adorned in a silvery light,
As shadows dance softly, bidding goodnight.
Stitched with the breezes that carry the day,
In patchwork dreams, all worries decay.

Every moment captured, like petals in bloom,
Beneath the cold moon, there's warmth in the gloom.
Threads of laughter linger, in air woven tight,
In fields of frost magic, we find pure delight.

With the rising sun, a new tale will spin,
In patchwork dreams, hope whispers within.
Together we wander, through frost and through dreams,
Life's richness revealed in the quiet of beams.

Stitches of a Longing Heart

In twilight's glow, the shadows meet,
Whispers of love in silence sweet.
Each stitch I weave, a hope reborn,
For every dream that I have worn.

Threads of sorrow, yet golden seams,
Telling tales of broken dreams.
With needle's grace, I mend my soul,
One stitch at a time, I feel whole.

In the fabric where wishes lie,
I can almost hear the sigh.
Each patchwork square a memory,
Crafted gently, setting me free.

The longing heart finds its own art,
Binding pieces, never apart.
With every stitch, my spirit heals,
In the quilt of love, the heart reveals.

Hibernation of Old Dreams

In the quiet of winter's breath,
Hopes lie still, held close to death.
Under layers of snow and ice,
Old aspirations slowly suffice.

Wrapped in shadows, dreams retreat,
In the silence, I find my seat.
Like whispers lost in frosty air,
They linger softly, filled with care.

Yet deep beneath the frozen ground,
A spark of life is still around.
As winter wanes, they will awake,
From slumber deep, no more ache.

With the thaw, the colors bloom,
Creating joy to chase the gloom.
Hibernation ends, and I find,
Old dreams refreshed, no longer blind.

Fabric of Forgotten Lullabies

In twilight's warmth, the lullabies fade,
Once sung softly, memories made.
Whispers of night, a gentle caress,
Filling the heart, a sweet recess.

Threads of silk, spun from the past,
Echoes of love forever cast.
Stitched in layers of time and care,
Forgotten songs linger in the air.

In every stitch, a story lives,
A fabric woven with tender gives.
Holding moments in the seams tight,
Lullabies whisper through the night.

Though silence reigns, the echoes flow,
In every fiber, the feelings grow.
A quilt of dreams, a tapestry,
The lullabies hum in harmony.

Memories Sewn with Winterlight

In the shimmering frost of dawn,
Memories gather, tenderly drawn.
Each moment wrapped in crystal white,
Sewn together with winterlight.

Softly they glow, the past in view,
Hues of nostalgia, a haunting hue.
Warmth of the heart in muted shade,
In the fabric of time, love is laid.

Winter's breath hums a soothing tune,
Creating warmth where shadows loom.
Stitch by stitch, I weave the time,
Through chilly nights and perfect rhyme.

As seasons shift, the threads remain,
Tales of joy, a touch of pain.
Memories glisten, held so tight,
In the quilt woven with winterlight.

Snowy Threads of Delight

Flakes descend, soft and white,
Dancing gently in the light.
Whispers of joy fill the air,
A winter's magic, pure and rare.

Children laugh with glee and cheer,
Creating snowmen, drawing near.
Sleds slide down the hills with grace,
In this snowy, enchanted place.

Each breath a puff, warm and bright,
Hands turned red from the chilly bite.
A world transformed, so pure and bright,
Snowy threads weave pure delight.

As night falls soft, stars ignite,
The moon bathes all in silver light.
Under blankets, stories unfold,
Of snowy nights and dreams retold.

Stitched Stories of Frost

Winter weaves a tale so cold,
Frosty threads in silver bold.
Each branch dressed, a crystal gown,
In this quiet, sleepy town.

Footprints echo, stories told,
Adventures shared, both new and old.
With every step, memories blend,
Stitched in laughter, love, and friends.

As the sun dips low and red,
Soft blankets wrap the earth, it's said.
The silence deep, a lullaby,
Frosty tales beneath the sky.

In twilight's hush, we gather near,
With whispered wishes, dreams appear.
Stitched stories in the frosty air,
Of winter's charm, beyond compare.

Warm Threads of Nostalgia

In winter's chill, we find the glow,
Of memories wrapped in soft warm flow.
Laughter echoes in candlelight,
As we recall those cozy nights.

Grandma's quilt, a treasured frame,
Stitched with love, it feels the same.
The scent of cocoa, sweet and rich,
Hugs that comfort, hearts that stitch.

Fireside talks, the shadows play,
A tapestry of yesterday.
Warm threads weave through time like gold,
Stories cherished, gently told.

As snowflakes dance and softly fall,
We hold the warmth of tales, our all.
In every thread, a hug so tight,
Nostalgia glows in winter's night.

Patchwork of Silent Snow

A patchwork quilt of silent snow,
Blanketing the earth below.
Each flake unique, a soft design,
Nature's canvas, pure and fine.

Trees adorned in white attire,
Whisper secrets, never tire.
The world appears a softer place,
In this quiet, frozen embrace.

Footsteps muffled, soft and slow,
Worn paths where only few will go.
In stillness found, we pause and breathe,
Patchwork dreams that winter weaves.

As night descends, stars shine bright,
Guiding us with gentle light.
Silent snow, a calming bliss,
In its purity, we find our peace.

The Threads That Hold Us Close

In whispered tones beneath the stars,
We weave our dreams, no matter how far.
Each heart a stitch, in a quilt so wide,
Together we stand, a love undenied.

Through storms that rage and shadows deep,
We gather close, our secrets to keep.
The threads entwine, a vibrant dance,
In every glance, a shared romance.

From laughter's spark to sorrow's sigh,
We hold each other as time slips by.
In every moment, let love prevail,
Our bonds are strong, they never fail.

With every sunrise, a brand new start,
Together we mend each fragile heart.
In this tapestry, we find our way,
The threads that hold us, day by day.

Fables of Frost on Willow Lane

In winter's grip, where willows weep,
The frost tells tales of secrets deep.
With every breath, the stories flow,
Of love once lost, of hearts aglow.

Each branch adorned with sparkling frost,
Recalls the warmth of what we've lost.
Beneath the stillness, whispers rise,
Of dreams that linger beneath grey skies.

Children laugh in the shimmering light,
Their footprints dance, a joyful sight.
Through empty fields and snowy glades,
Fables of frost, where memory fades.

On Willow Lane, where echoes play,
The stories linger, night and day.
In every shadow, history stays,
A frozen canvas of love's embrace.

Fabrics of Family and Frost

In cozy corners where warmth resides,
We stitch together so many sides.
With threads of laughter and tears combined,
The fabrics of family are intertwined.

When winter calls with its icy breath,
We gather close, defying death.
Each moment shared, a pattern spun,
In the tapestry of life, we are one.

With stories told by the fireside glow,
The frost outside can't steal our show.
In every heartbeat, a thread is drawn,
Creating a bond that will carry on.

Together we weave, through thick and thin,
In family's fabric, we all fit in.
With joy and love as our guiding light,
We'll face the frost, emerge from the night.

Legacy of a Forgotten Hearth

In the stillness, where ashes rest,
Whispers tell of a time blessed.
A hearth once warm, now cold as stone,
Holds a legacy we've all outgrown.

Memories linger, like smoke in air,
Echoes of laughter that used to share.
Footsteps fade in the dust of time,
While stories remain, in rhythm and rhyme.

Through crumbling walls, the sunlight streams,
Igniting the shadows of shattered dreams.
Each corner holds a life once lived,
A treasure trove of love, freely given.

Yet hope prevails, as seasons change,
From forgotten past, our lives rearrange.
In every ember, a spark ignites,
The legacy lives, through days and nights.

A Canvas of Snowswept Love

In silence, the snowflakes dance and twirl,
A soft white blanket 'round each pearl.
Hearts entwined 'neath the silver sky,
Whispers of warmth in a frosty sigh.

Together we carve our names in the frost,
In this winter realm, no love is lost.
Each breath creates clouds that gently fade,
In the canvas of love, memories are laid.

The hush of the night, a tender embrace,
Embracing the chill with a lover's grace.
Beneath the stars, dreams come alive,
In the depths of winter, our spirits thrive.

So let the world frost, and the cold winds blight,
In this snowswept love, we find our light.
With hearts unburdened, we shall remain,
A canvas of snowswept love, eternal refrain.

Rustic Dreams in a Frozen Frame

Wood smoke rising on frosty air,
Gentle whispers of winters rare.
Crisp leaves crunch beneath our feet,
A rustic charm where memories meet.

Old barns stand proud with coats of white,
Holding secrets through the long, cold night.
In the glow of lanterns, spirits roam,
In every corner, we find our home.

Snowdrifts piled high like dreams untold,
Still and solid, the stories unfold.
Wrapped in blankets by the fireside,
Rustic dreams in hearts abide.

With each sip of cocoa, laughter flows,
In this frozen frame, our love only grows.
Together we cherish the life we design,
In every frozen breath, our hearts align.

Lullabies of the Loom

Threads of warmth entwined in grace,
In quiet corners, we find our space.
The loom sings softly, weaving delight,
Lullabies that dance with the night.

Colors swirl in a tender embrace,
Each stitch a memory, a cherished place.
With gentle hands, we craft our dreams,
In threads of hope, our heartstrings gleam.

The tapestry grows, stories unfold,
Of laughter and warmth, legends retold.
Each fiber carries a whisper of love,
In this woven world, a gift from above.

As night gently falls, we rest our heads,
Wrapped in comfort, where love spreads.
With lullabies soft, the stars appear,
In the loom of our lives, forever near.

The Toast of Seasons Past

Glasses raised to the days gone by,
To autumn's gold and winter's sky.
Each clink a story, each sip a song,
In the toast of seasons, we all belong.

Memories linger like cinnamon spice,
Moments shared, oh so nice.
Time flows softly, like a gentle stream,
In the warmth of memories, we find our dream.

From spring's first blooms to summer's heat,
The journey continues, life bittersweet.
Through laughter and tears, we carve our path,
In the toast of seasons, a heartfelt laugh.

So gather 'round for the tales we tell,
In each season's spirit, we weave our spell.
Toast to the memories, both far and near,
In the dance of the seasons, we hold them dear.

Fleeting Moments in Cotton Dreams

In twilight's grasp, the whispers sway,
Cotton clouds drift, then fade away.
Silent laughter in the air,
Moments twinkle, light as prayer.

Softly woven in twilight's seam,
Each heartbeat flutters like a dream.
Wishes carried on a breeze,
Time suspends, then bends with ease.

Sugar-coated hopes arise,
Underneath the watchful skies.
Memories dance on cotton threads,
In this world where nothing dreads.

Fleeting frames in soft embrace,
Cascading time, a tender grace.
In the dusk, we find our way,
Cotton dreams that brightly play.

The Warmth of Faded Wishes

Beneath the stars, my wishes glow,
Softly fading, yet they know.
Echoes of a distant past,
Woven dreams that strive to last.

Whispers of the heart, so warm,
Faded wishes take their form.
Memories knit in twilight's hue,
The warmth remains, though dreams are few.

Time may weather, spirit free,
In the quiet, you'll find me.
Gathered hope in silver light,
Faded wishes take to flight.

Cradled dreams, they softly hum,
Reminding me where I am from.
In the silence, hear the sound,
Of faded wishes, love profound.

Treasures from the Frosty Past

In winter's grasp, the whispers call,
Frosty jewels that softly fall.
Memories wrapped in icy lace,
Time's embrace, a tender grace.

Glimmers of light through frosted glass,
Treasures lost, yet held fast.
Silent stories, hearts intertwined,
In frozen echoes, warmth we find.

From bitter winds, a solace grows,
In quietude, the spirit knows.
Fragments of joy in the stillness rest,
Frosty past, you are a guest.

Glistening moments, again they gleam,
Woven tightly like a dream.
In the chill, the heart beats bold,
Treasures in the frost, pure gold.

Tangles of Yarn and Memory

A skein of thoughts in twilight spun,
Tangles of yarn 'neath the setting sun.
Every twist, a story told,
In threads of silver, hints of gold.

Knots of laughter, sighs entwined,
In every fiber, love confined.
Weaving moments, heart to heart,
Tangled memories never part.

Through tangled paths, we find our way,
In the warmth of every stay.
Yarn of time that softly bends,
A tapestry that never ends.

From tangled skeins, new patterns rise,
In shadows deep, the spirit flies.
Each thread, a whisper, a gentle plea,
In tangled yarn, there's harmony.

Snowflake Remembrances

Each flake a whisper, soft and light,
Dancing in the chill of the night.
A memory brushed on winter's breath,
Fragile beauty, a moment's wreath.

They swirl and twirl in moon's soft glow,
Carrying stories from long ago.
Silent wishes drift and play,
In the heart of cold, they find their way.

Every crystal tells a tale,
Of frost-kissed dreams that will not pale.
In the hush of the falling snow,
Lies the warmth of love's gentle glow.

Hold close these fleeting, icy signs,
For in each flake, the past aligns.
Snowflake remembrances in the air,
A treasure trove of moments rare.

Heirlooms of the Heart

In faded boxes, treasures hide,
Whispers of love through the ages bide.
Threads of laughter, stitches of tears,
Woven together through all the years.

Each piece a token, a story spun,
Heavy with memories, weighed with fun.
Fragile as dreams, yet strong as the sun,
Crafted with care, where life's threads run.

The quilt of our past wraps around tight,
With colors that shimmer, both dark and bright.
In moments of sorrow, in joy so sweet,
Our heirlooms of heart make us complete.

So hold it close, this cherished lore,
In every stitch, feel love's encore.
Heirlooms remind us of who we are,
Guiding us home, like a distant star.

Blanketed in Time

The world is wrapped in a quilt of white,
Each flake a memory — soft, polite.
Time stands still, in glittering frost,
In this serene moment, we find what's lost.

Gentle silence envelops the land,
Creating a canvas, vast and grand.
Footprints reveal where we've walked before,
Each step a story, each breath a score.

As stars twinkle in the midnight sky,
Nature whispers, a gentle sigh.
Blanketed in time, we pause and reflect,
In snow's vast embrace, we find our respect.

Memories drift on the winter's air,
A tapestry woven with love and care.
Blanketed in time, when hearts align,
In the hush of winter, we feel divine.

The Cozy Embrace of Winter's Tale

Inside the hearth, the flames dance bright,
Casting shadows that flicker with light.
Wrapped in blankets, hearts intertwine,
In winter's embrace, all feels just fine.

The world outside is cold and bare,
But here within, there's warmth to share.
Each laughter echoes, a melodic ring,
In cozy corners, memories spring.

The scent of spices and sweet delight,
Fills the air on this peaceful night.
We gather close, telling tales of old,
In the cozy embrace, our hearts unfold.

As snowflakes dance in a swirling spree,
We cherish this moment, just you and me.
The winter's tale whispers soft and slow,
In its cozy embrace, our love will grow.

Memories Harvested in Frost

In the quiet field, frost lays down,
Whispers of laughter, a forgotten sound.
Footprints traced in icy grace,
Echoes of moments time can't erase.

Beneath silver skies, memories grow,
Each flake a story, each freeze a glow.
Wrapped in the chill, we hold what's true,
Frosty reminders of me and you.

Echoes of Fabric Beneath the Stars

In the soft night, fabrics intertwine,
Stories whispered in the threads divine.
Under the blanket of twinkling light,
Echoes of dreams take magnificent flight.

Patterns of laughter, colors of tears,
Stitched together through all of the years.
Beneath the cosmos, every seam glows,
A tapestry woven with love that flows.

Tales from Under the Snowdrift

Beneath the white, secrets softly breathe,
Tales of the earth, mysteries we weave.
Snowdrifts conceal what stories they hold,
As whispers of winter, quietly told.

Branches bow low, adorned in the chill,
Crafting each tale with a whispering thrill.
As snowflakes dance, a world comes alive,
In the stillness, past memories thrive.

The Weave of Yesterday's Hues

In twilight's glow, colors collide,
Yesterday's whispers in shades abide.
Threads of a past that time can't forego,
Weaving the hues of the life we know.

Sunset's embrace, a canvas so grand,
Paints of our journeys, by hearts, they're planned.
Strokes of regret, and joy intertwined,
In this vibrant weave, we're forever enshrined.

Woven Wishes Under Snow

Silvery whispers dance on air,
Dreams scatter softly, unaware.
Footsteps trace the frozen ground,
In each flake, a wish is found.

Stars blink through the blanket white,
Guiding hearts through winter's night.
Wrapped in silence, hope takes flight,
Woven wishes, pure delight.

Branches bow under the weight,
Secrets held by snow's embrace.
Every crystal tells a tale,
Of love and warmth that will prevail.

As dawn breaks with golden hue,
Promises bloom, fresh and new.
Beneath the chill, a fire glows,
In woven wishes, life still flows.

Tapestry of Yearning and Chill

Threads of longing weave the night,
Hushed in shadows, dreams take flight.
Fingers trace the patterns near,
In the fabric, warmth draws near.

Winds of winter call my name,
Echoes whisper, love's sweet game.
Hearts entwined in icy lace,
Yearning glimmers, time won't erase.

Each stitch binds the stories told,
Wrapped in frost, yet brave and bold.
Light streams through the woven seams,
We build our world from frosted dreams.

As the cold begins to fade,
Hope ignites where shadows played.
In this tapestry we find,
Chill and warmth, forever intertwined.

Threads of Frosted Reminiscence

Frosted memories rise like smoke,
Softly drifting, silent cloak.
Every breath a fleeting past,
Whispers echo, shadows cast.

In the stillness, stories sleep,
Woven deep, their secrets keep.
Time unravels with the dawn,
In the threads, we carry on.

Through the chill, a warmth remains,
Guiding us through joy and pains.
In every stitch, the heart recalls,
Life's embrace, where love enthralls.

Frosted reminiscing so sweet,
Every heartbeat, every beat.
Together we shall find our way,
In threads of frost, we ever stay.

The Warmth Beneath the Ice

Beneath the surface, embers glow,
Hidden warmth, in the depths below.
Winter's grip may try to bind,
But in the heart, love's light we find.

Crystals glisten, cold and bright,
Yet within, a fierce delight.
Every layer we must traverse,
Holds a promise, deep and terse.

As the sun begins to rise,
Melting dreams and hopeful sighs.
Through the thaw, new life created,
Frosted paths, now liberating.

Underneath the frozen guise,
A universe of love that lies.
The warmth beneath, our guiding star,
No matter how distant we are.

Milton Keynes UK
Ingram Content Group UK Ltd.
UKHW021846151124
451262UK00014B/1313